PRAISE FOR PROPERO PARTNERS' TRAINING MATERIALS

"Excellent content—has provoked some thought and would be interested in how Propero could help us move forward with our marketing strategy and growing our business over the coming years"
—*P. Millward, Director ABtec*

"The information was well laid out and gave good insight as to how to convert clients"
—*K. Sawford, New Business Sales Jumpstart UK*

"Took away some good tips and advice on marketing that I'll be putting into action asap!"
—*E. Fontoura, Solicitor Advocate Broadgate Legal*

"Thanks Propero for a very enjoyable event—look forward to the next one!"
—*P. Noyce, Partner Menzies LLP*

AS FEATURED IN:

The Times, The Guardian, City A.M., Solicitors Journal

Cover design: Vanessa Kerr
Content design: Vanessa Kerr

© 2018 Propero Partners

Published by Propero Partners, 14 Gower's Walk
London E1 8PY

www.properopartners.com

No part of this publication may be reproduced, stored in a retrieval system, or transmitted in any form or by any means, electronic, mechanical, photocopying, recording, scanning, or otherwise, without the prior written permission of the Publisher.

P.

Preface	p.5
About The Authors	p.9
Introduction	p.10
1. Why Social Media?	p.12
2. Choosing The Right Social Media Platforms For Your Firm	p.16
3. Social Optimisation: Making The Most Of Your Social Profiles	p.38
4. Key Social Media Takeaways To Action Today	p.55
5. Achieve Your Business Goals With Marketing	p.58
6. Know When to Stop Doing It Yourself	p.70
Social Media Calendar	p.83

PREFACE

"Can social media *actually* help grow my business?", it's a question we hear time and again through our work at Propero Partners.

While social media is just one of the myriad digital marketing tactics we employ to deliver right-fit leads to our clients, it's one that's getting a lot more airtime as Gen X-ers (now more commonly known as millennials) grow into senior decision-making roles and fill seats in boardrooms.

Many of the professional services firms we work with—across the legal, accountancy, finance, management consultancy and IT consultancy industries—were bewildered and sceptical of the subject at first. Social media has become a bit of an ugly sister compared to other digital marketing activities.

Many of the firms that we've spoken to—at training events, after downloading a white paper, that reached out to an account manager or those that have come through our doors on Gower's Walk in London—have tried social media for themselves. And the experience they've had leads them to believe that social media isn't quite right for them. They don't see how their tweet could possibly stand out amongst the haze of product placements and cat videos, let alone generate new business.

While not all platforms are made equal, there are gains to be made from social media. In June 2017, we launched our annual report (The State of Digital Marketing in Professional Services) with findings from over 370 senior decision-makers in professional services industries and their approach to generating new business enquiries and referrals. In the report we concluded that these firms are utilising all areas of marketing, including email marketing, social media, marketing budgets, lead generation and so on...

One of the key research findings? Professionals and firms in traditional industries ARE active on social media. While it may seem like firms in professional services aren't online, our research shows that they are actively engaging in conversations on social media with right-fit clients.

Firms in the legal industry, especially, are more aggressive with their online marketing tactics - and professionals in other industries, such as accountancy and management consultancy, are more active in a personal capacity.

This means the firms that are failing to get on board with a social media plan are effectively lining the pockets of their competitors.

Our research findings led us to write the Marketing for Non-Marketers series, to share our advice and inform professional services firms on the value of digital marketing to grow their businesses in the digital age.

In this short book, we will discuss our learnings from a foundational level—from choosing the right social media platforms for your firm, to consistently optimising your social media presence—to ensure you have the tools you need to get started with social media.

For a deeper level of understanding, keep your eyes peeled for upcoming books in the series.

Niamh Hickey
Junior Marketing Manager

ABOUT THE AUTHORS

MELISSA HERNANDEZ focuses on B2B social media marketing for Propero. She makes it possible for businesses to boost their reach and social presence, to hold their own in crowded industries. She's an expert at writing, planning, and producing content across all social media channels, with a drive to increase follower-base and social footprint.

NIAMH HICKEY holds a first class honours master's degree in International Entrepreneurship Management. While managing a team of digital marketing experts, Niamh identifies strategic growth opportunities and executes end-to-end digital marketing campaigns to achieve results for small and medium-sized businesses.

BETH KAYSER drives day-to-day online content creation and strategy. Beth's ethos is to challenge, improve and move forward—an approach that keeps her abreast of ever-changing content and distribution methods. This knowledge helps her and the wider team produce future-facing, relevant content for clients, which in turn positions them as the obvious choice in front of leads.

KELLY O'CONNOR is a business development and digital marketing expert who specialises in delivering long-term value for businesses. She builds strong relationships with her clients, and provides ongoing contact and strategic support to guide them through marketing campaigns that yield measurable results.

INTRODUCTION

Today, you'll buy a stale cheese sandwich from your local station kiosk and feel the urge to share a piece of it with the rest of the world. Taking a photograph or penning a recommendation to share on social media, however simple it may seem, is a means of creating and distributing new content. And in today's world, it has become almost second nature and it doesn't show signs of letting up any time soon.

If you can record it on your phone (or whatever the latest handheld device is), chances are, you'll quickly upload it to your preferred social network (LinkedIn, Facebook, Twitter, Instagram). This is so your work peers, family or a group that shares a similar interest to you, can see and comment on it.

And if you don't feel the same way, you're among the shrinking few.

This obsession with over-documenting EVERYTHING (the mundane to the unbelievable) has led to a surge in the amount of digital content available. New platforms are emerging every day to facilitate our need for a constant flow of images, videos and stories. Not only that, but with the advent of live streaming and instant media, we've become accustomed to receiving our news as soon as it breaks.

We, the public, are information hungry and we've a growing desire for 'fauxperiences'. We want to be able to listen to it, or watch it unfold without actually being there. We want to taste it before we sit down to eat it, gaining 'first-hand' experience before we actually try it for ourselves.

This equates to much more than a generation of mobile zombies with lessening attention spans and a growing impatience for shoddy content. This means the environment in which your firm operates is changing, every single day.

Traditional, disruptive marketing is out.

Consumers have learned to tune out the white noise of ads on an endless rotation and instead recognise that they have the power, the voice and the know-how to learn everything they want to know about your firm—not just what you cherry-pick to tell them. And with a simple swipe of a screen and touch of a button, he or she can share their opinion with millions.

Although consumer power can seem daunting, the evolution of the online platform has afforded us an even playing field. You and Mr. Consumer have the same tools right at your fingertips...

The question is, why aren't you using them to your advantage?

CHAPTER 1

WHY SOCIAL MEDIA?

Today, no marketing plan is complete without a social media strategy.

Making use of current technology, you can focus on the platforms your best-fit clients are most engaged with to speed up the delivery of your marketing messages.

But all activity must be profitable. Avoid the temptation to use technology just because it exists, and instead demand each platform you use provides measurable, proven results.

Social media has a multitude of different, overcomplicated definitions. In our opinion, the most true and reflective comes from The Oxford Dictionary, which describes social media as:

"Websites and applications that enable users to create and share content or to participate in social networking."

> **2.06 BILLION FACEBOOK ACTIVE USERS**
>
> **700 MILLION INSTAGRAM ACTIVE USERS**
>
> **328 MILLION TWITTER ACTIVE USERS**
>
> **106 MILLION LINKEDIN ACTIVE USERS**
>
> *- Statista, September 2017*

What does that mean? **Unlimited opportunity!**

What we often hear, when approaching the topic of social media with our clients, is that it isn't for professional services, isn't necessary for B2B businesses, and will take too much time to keep up.

There's no doubt that getting the most out of social media takes time, effort and patience but, when used in the right way, you *will* see rewards.

In the current, hyper-competitive marketplace, businesses need to be visible, available and open to conversations across all lines of communication. Your right-fit prospects expect to be able to consume content whenever and wherever they choose.

Companies that don't have a social presence will always be one step behind those that do. Being active on social platforms means giving potential clients another avenue to engage with your brand. Not only that, but you can extract insights from their social media activity to better understand the pain points and issues affecting their industry and business.

Not just in the context of social media, but with all marketing, you should stop thinking of your clients as 'businesses'. Regardless of whether your services are B2B or B2C, you should be marketing in a H2H (human-to-human) way.

Think about it—behind every business there will be key decision-makers who are on **at least** one social platform, whether that's for professional reasons or to see pictures of their niece on her gap year. It doesn't matter whether they have a business account or a personal one, every platform they're on opens up another channel of communication, which means another opportunity to put your services in front of them.

Striking the balance between getting your message across in a meaningful way and bombarding your audience with endless, unengaging posts, takes skill and understanding. And one of the trickiest decisions to make is deciding when and where to start... especially when there are over 60 social channels worldwide, waiting to be utilised.

It's impossible (not to mention a waste of time) to be active on all social platforms at any one time. Before doing anything, take the time to research and understand which social channels your audience—be that existing or prospective clients—are active on. Once you've established this, you'll have a better idea of which platforms your business should prioritise.

82% OF FIRMS BELONG TO LINKEDIN, 64% TO TWITTER AND 55% TO FACEBOOK.

We also asked respondents which social networks they personally belong to. 85% said LinkedIn, 62% Twitter and 72% Facebook.

- UK INDUSTRY REPORT 2017
The State of Digital Marketing in Professional Services

CHAPTER 2

CHOOSING THE RIGHT SOCIAL MEDIA PLATFORMS FOR YOUR FIRM

Once you know where your target audience is engaged online, you can make an informed decision on where *your firm* should be present.

As we mentioned earlier, there are over 60 social platforms to choose from. Don't overwhelm yourself; pick two or three to start with. As a good jumping-off point, we recommend setting up LinkedIn and Facebook accounts to our professional services clients who are just starting out on social media.

LinkedIn is a social platform that focuses on all things business and employment. It's the most 'professional' of all the social channels and boasts 467 million business men, women and company profiles globally (Statista, 2017). When used correctly, LinkedIn has the ability to get your firm in front of a highly engaged, business-focused audience.

> **50% of B2B buyers use LinkedIn when making purchasing decisions**
>
> **7/10 professionals describe the platform as a trustworthy source of professional content**

- Hootsuite, 2016

In the professional services industry, if a prospective client has just one social media profile, it's going to be LinkedIn. It's the world's largest professional network, which is why it's often at the heart of B2B social media marketing strategies.

The professionals using the platform are actively searching and engaging with its user-generated content on a daily basis, which means you have an opportunity to contribute valuable content that resonates with your audience through your business profile. In a survey conducted by the platform, it was found that 50% of B2B buyers use LinkedIn when making purchasing decisions, with 7/10 professionals describing the platform as a trustworthy source of professional content (Hootsuite, 2016). So, if you're unsure on where to start, LinkedIn is a safe bet.

Facebook might seem like an odd second choice for professional services firms, but we recommend it with good reason. It has more users than any other social platform (by a long stretch) totalling 2.06 billion (Statista, 2017). That's almost one in every five people on the planet!

Facebook is traditionally known to be used in more personal capacities, but in recent years the platform has developed improved services for owners of business pages. Ad campaigns, sponsored content and boosted posts have attracted interest from businesses across all industries. In fact, in 2015, Facebook announced it had over 50 million business pages, a number predicted only to increase in the years to come. So, when our suggestion for building a Facebook presence is met with scepticism, our reasoning is simple: Facebook is too big to ignore! Facebook is where everyone is—the humans behind the businesses you're targeting—which again means you have an opportunity to market in a human-to-human way.

CASE STUDY

B2B brands often struggle when it comes to creating buzz about their service because, let's face it, a B2B offering often isn't the most exciting thing to see on the internet.

But, if you take a closer look, you'll notice that the B2B brands utilising social media in a clever way, can and do see the kind of engagement we're all striving for... even without a conventionally 'exciting' business offering.

Take Maersk Line, for example. This container shipping company refused to accept that stifled yawns and wandering attention spans was their lot. Instead, they put their heads together to figure out a way they could make container shipping interesting to their target audience.

→

Their social media presence spans a number of platforms. In particular, their Facebook presence gives the brand credibility and sheds light on the humans behind their brand. They achieve this by posting both positive and negative news. For example, a description of when a ship of theirs hit a whale. It quickly became their most shared post on the page, and received mainly positive comments. They also share users' and employees' images.

By thinking outside the container (sorry, we had to) they've created a visual and relatable social media presence, and as a result, see very respectable engagement. With over 1.1 million followers on their Facebook page alone, this B2B brand is a perfect example of how social media can be used to market any service!

Depending on who you talk to, and the resources you have, Twitter is also a good platform for your firm to consider. One of Twitter's unique selling points (USPs) is that you can see the online conversations people are having, as they're having them.

A hashtag is a word or phrase preceded by a hash sign (#). It is used on social media sites and applications (especially Twitter) to identify messages on a specific topic. Following #hashtags on Twitter allows people from all over the globe to join in on 'hot topic' conversations.

At the heart of its function, each Twitter user is shown tailored trending hashtags. These show the conversations with the most contributions. It's a list that can be altered based on location or tailored to your interests, and a great tool for keeping your finger on the pulse of what's going on in the minds of your audience.

TWITTER'S LIST OF MOST TALKED ABOUT TOPICS IN EUROPE IN 2016 WERE:

#RIO2016
#ELECTION2016
#pokemongo *#EURO2016*
#OSCARS

EXPERT TIP: NO.1

The year's top trending hashtags give you an idea of the most talked about events. Some will naturally be more relevant to B2B industries than others. A successful social media marketer will be able to spot relevant trends and adapt existing content to fit those trends. It's all about staying on top of what your audience is talking about, and being active in the conversations they're already having. By doing so you're extending the reach of your brand voice.

IN
EDIN
FACE
BOO

HOW TO SET UP YOUR...

LINKEDIN

LinkedIn's support pages provide clear and easy-to-follow step-by-step guides on the logistics of setting up a LinkedIn account and company page. **To begin, you'll need to consider the following elements that will help you build your company page:**

(Later on we'll go through how to optimise all of your social profiles to get the most from your audiences).

- **Add a profile photo:** Usually this is your company logo as it makes your firm easily identifiable. *Did you know?* Companies with logo profile images get six times more visits to their company pages (LinkedIn, 2017)

- **Add a banner image:** This image only displays when someone clicks on to your page. It should fit within your brand guidelines (e.g. colours, fonts etc.) and be consistent with your overall online presence

- **Share your address:** Having your address on your firm's LinkedIn page will help to marry your physical and online presence

- **Write a short 'About us' section:** This should introduce other likeminded professionals to your company. Unlike Facebook and Twitter, your 'About us' on LinkedIn can be longer and should be a more formal representation of your services

- **Add your company details:** At a basic level, the company details you should include are: a link to your website, the industry in which you operate, and where you are headquartered.

EXPERT TIP: NO.2

You need to have a personal profile for Facebook or LinkedIn in order to set up a business page in either platform, as business pages require at least one 'admin'.

Propero Partners

Marketing and Advertising • London • 503 followers

2 connections work here. See all 7 employees on LinkedIn →

Manage page | **See jobs**

About us

STRATEGIC MARKETING FOR BUSINESSES IN TRADITIONAL INDUSTRIES

At Propero Partners, we design and implement strategic marketing campaigns to establish a point of difference for our clients in traditional industries.

For many businesses in traditional industries, reputation used to be enough. But, gone are the days of depending on word-of-mouth referrals. If your business isn't being found by the people who are actively looking for the services you offer, you're losing prospective clients to your competitors every day.

The Propero team has been helping businesses like yours experience real, predictable growth for decades. Our flawlessly executed marketing processes ensure that you're not only found when people are searching for what it is you offer, but that you're found first.

If you want to stand out as a leader in your industry, attract a consistent stream of your ideal clients and plan for predictable business growth…

We can help.

Company details

Website
http://www.ProperoPartners.com

Headquarters
London

Company type
Privately Held

Company size
11-50 employees

Specialties
legal marketing, professional services marketing, financial services marketing, accountancy marketing, consultancy marketing, and IT consultancy marketing

Recent update   See all

What to expect from Philip Hammond's …
businessinsider.com

37m

HOW TO SET UP YOUR...

FACEBOOK

Just like LinkedIn, Facebook Blueprint provides clear and easy-to-follow step-by-step guides on the logistics of setting up a Facebook account and business page.

To create your business page, you'll need to implement the following:

- **An appropriate profile image:** Ideally, this should be your firm's logo. Your profile image will be shown alongside your posts when they appear on your audience's feed so it needs to be identifiable

- **Branded cover image:** Choose an image that represents your firm in a more personal way. Facebook is a platform people use to interact socially (rather than professionally) so your choice of image should reflect that.

- **Write a short bio:** Add a short bio to your page. This should be no more than a couple of sentences which sum up the mission of your business

- **Tell your story:** This is your opportunity to explain what sets your firm apart from others in the industry. This can be longer than the bio as it doesn't appear on your profile page, so you can include ~10 sentences

- **Pick a username:** Create a username to make it easier for people to find your company page. Make sure it's easily recognisable so it appears when someone searches for your firm

Under the 'About' section:

- **Add your contact details:** Including your business address, contact number and a support email address such as: *info@yourcompanyname.com*

- **And a website link:** Make it easy for followers to find your website. Doing so legitimises your page and ties your online presence together.

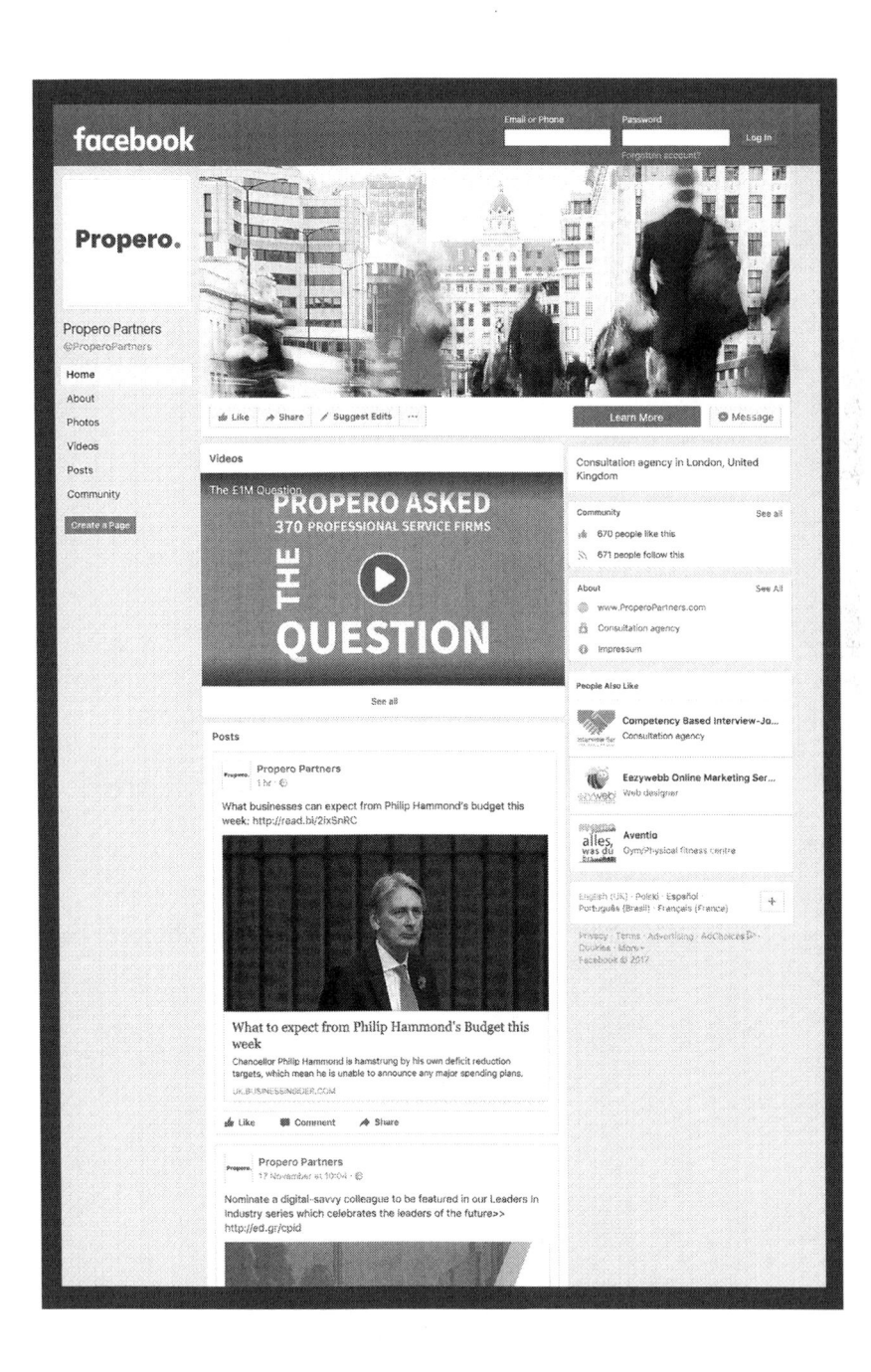

facebook

Email or Phone | Password | Log In
Forgotten account?

Propero.

Propero Partners
@ProperoPartners

- Home
- About
- Photos
- Videos
- Posts
- Community

Create a Page

👍 Like   ↗ Share   ✏ Suggest Edits   ...   Learn More   ✉ Message

Videos

The £1M Question
PROPERO ASKED 370 PROFESSIONAL SERVICE FIRMS THE QUESTION

See all

Posts

Propero Partners
1 hr

What businesses can expect from Philip Hammond's budget this week: http://read.bi/2ixSnRC

What to expect from Philip Hammond's Budget this week
Chancellor Philip Hammond is hamstrung by his own deficit reduction targets, which mean he is unable to announce any major spending plans.
UK.BUSINESSINSIDER.COM

👍 Like   💬 Comment   ↗ Share

Propero Partners
17 November at 10:04

Nominate a digital-savvy colleague to be featured in our Leaders in Industry series which celebrates the leaders of the future>>
http://ed.gr/cpid

Consultation agency in London, United Kingdom

Community   See all
👍 670 people like this
🔖 671 people follow this

About   See All
🌐 www.ProperoPartners.com
🏢 Consultation agency
ⓘ Impressum

People Also Like

🤝 **Competency Based Interview-Jo...**
Consultation agency

🌐 **Eezywebb Online Marketing Ser...**
Web designer

Aventia
Gym/Physical fitness centre

English (UK) · Polski · Español ·
Português (Brasil) · Français (France)   +

Privacy · Terms · Advertising · AdChoices ▷ ·
Cookies · More ·
Facebook © 2017

HOW TO SET UP YOUR...

TWITTER

As a social platform, Twitter acts as the go-to place for bite-size news. Take the BBC's Twitter presence as an example. Twitter enables the BBC to update people in real-time, as events are happening and, as a result, the BBC tweets at least once every 10 minutes. Therefore what you promote on Twitter and the way you do it, should align with the platform.

To set up your firm's page, follow the steps outlined by Twitter. **We've covered the basics below:**

- **Choose an appropriate username:** Make sure you are easily-identifiable when someone searches your firm's name. It would look something like: @yourbusinessname

- **Select a profile image:** It's best practise to make this your company's logo because this image will be shown next to all of your posts

- **And a header image:** This is the image that appears at the top of your profile. You can change this as often as you like but it should align with your firm's branding

- **Write a short bio:** Remember Twitter is usually reserved for news, so keep this short and snappy. Summarise your business in one sentence with no industry jargon.

While some firms in professional services choose to ignore the benefits of maintaining a social media presence, many have learned to engage with prospective clients and to drive revenue from online business.

This is a sure sign that the momentum behind social media marketing isn't going to let up any time soon.

Propero.

Tweets	Following	Followers	Likes	Lists	Moments
1,446	418	450	137	0	0

Propero Partners
@ProperoUK

We design and implement strategic marketing campaigns that establish a point of difference for businesses in traditional industries.

◎ London
⚭ ProperoPartners.com
▦ Joined December 2014
▣ 593 Photos and videos

Tweets   Tweets & replies   Media

📌 Pinned Tweet

Propero Partners @ProperoUK · Nov 15
Last week, we published a piece (bit.ly/2zyFwc0) outlining the impact of #GDPR on B2B #marketing. Is your firm prepared? -Melissa

0% Yes, we're prepared
0% We're working on it
0% No, we won't be impacted
0% We're unsure

0 votes · 2 days left

Propero Partners @ProperoUK · 2h
What businesses can expect from Philip Hammond's budget this week:
reud.bi/2ixSnRC

77% of accountants use social media, according to the Wolters Kluwer Social Media Survey

- ICAEW, 2014

62% of law firms maintain a social presence when 35% of lawyers have obtained clients directly through their social networks

- ABA TechReport, 2014

Once you've set up your business pages across your chosen platforms, it's important to go beyond the basics and consider a 'marketing approach' to establish your online presence. This means thinking through your business' identity and brand values *(more on this in our Website Optimisation book)*, and how to best represent them online. Maintaining consistent branding will help your firm to become more recognisable and familiar, which will in turn encourage loyalty among your followers and generate further awareness.

Make it easy for consumers to recognise your business by maintaining consistency across the following areas:

- Brand personality is when **human traits are attributed to a brand** to make it more relatable to its target audience, and to help differentiate it from the competition. An effective brand increases its brand equity by having a consistent set of traits. To best portray your brand personality online, listen to how your audience communicates and how your competitors communicate with them—are they formal and precise; or casual and conversational? Based on your findings, put together a list of adjectives that best describe what resonates with your audience and how you want your business to be perceived. Whether it's authoritative, quick-witted, colloquial and chatty, formal, expert, straightforward, or rebellious—these are the personality traits your brand needs to embody in all of its visual and verbal communications

- Use the traits you've identified to guide your brand's voice, meaning the **tone of your communications**, and writing style. If you've chosen authoritative and expert traits to personify your brand, your written voice should be clear and definitive, e.g. you'll need to eliminate "just" and "maybe" from your copy, and your content is less likely to include abbreviations. It's also important to consider whether your brand will communicate as one whole, or use individual members of the team to add a personal touch

- Now use the voice and traits you've identified to **inform the topics your brand is passionate about** and the discussions your business will start/weigh-in on online. Consider your target audience: what are they interested in, and what do they care enough about to engage with on social media? Whether it's industry news, thought leadership or future technologies, a clear idea of what your business will AND won't discuss will ensure your business' company page only promotes posts that are interesting and relevant to its readership

- While you have most likely chosen and **established your brand colours** before setting up your online social media profiles, it's important to maintain that brand consistency across online and offline mediums. The colours you choose to represent your brand shouldn't relate to your individual preferences, but the kind of business you're in. For instance, bright blue colours are commonly used by tech firms, e.g. PayPal and Stripe, deep reds are often associated with politics or professional services, e.g. The Economist and PwC, while canary yellow and electric blue are often affiliated with discount offerings, e.g. Ryanair and IKEA. Incorporate your chosen brand colours where possible, for instance in the header image of your profile and in any images or visual posts distributed on your page's feed

- When creating **imagery and visuals to post on social media**, it's important to maintain consistency and ensure design is in line with the brand identity you've created. Consider the kind of photos your firm will share online, whether you favour a clean, simple aesthetic or a bold colour palette, you'll need to ensure your chosen look and feel is mirrored in both online and offline materials.

When exercised to its full potential, social media can be a *powerful* part of your client generation toolbox. It is one of the easiest and quickest ways to...

- Build authority and establish yourself as an industry expert
- Receive feedback on your offering
- Target specific buyers
- Generate new business

Not to mention boost visibility and awareness for your firm, at little cost to you.

But a simple Facebook page or Twitter account isn't going to increase your revenue overnight. You need to engage with your audience and inspire them to take action—like enquire when they need your services.

CHAPTER 3

SOCIAL OPTIMISATION: MAKING THE MOST OF YOUR SOCIAL PROFILES

Top performing professional services firms *are* investing time and effort into social media. In fact, according to Propero Partners' *State of Digital Marketing in the Professional Services Industry report (2017),* 54% of businesses that convert 45+ new enquiries a month use organic (free) social media.

However, like most things in life, you only get out what you put in. There's no point setting up social media profiles if they're going to gather dust—a neglected social media profile will give off a bad first impression to prospective clients. In fact, unattended social accounts actually do *more* harm than good. They send the message that either you don't have enough to talk about, or that you don't have the resources required to maintain them.

> **95% OF B2B MARKETERS HAVE CREATED CORPORATE SOCIAL MEDIA ACCOUNTS BUT HALF ARE STILL NOT ACTIVE ON SOCIAL MEDIA ON A REGULAR BASIS.**
>
> *- Meltwater, 2015*

So, now that you're set up with a LinkedIn, Facebook and Twitter page, we're going to outline what maintaining a successful B2B social media presence looks like in practise.

Although each platform is unique, there are some universal standards you should be meeting across **all social platforms** if you want to reach a larger audience and increase engagement with your posts.

BUILD AND MAINTAIN RELATIONSHIPS

While social media isn't a 'quick win,' when it comes to attracting new clients, a strong social presence has long-term value.

By actively engaging and interacting with other social media users, you will eventually build a pool of 'connections' (virtual relationships with likeminded people who are interested in what you have to say). Growing your following means you're increasing your brand's exposure, widening its audience and establishing a reputation.

For example, if an individual makes the effort to engage with your brand, either by liking, commenting on or sharing your content, or 'connecting' with you, you can (and should) respond by engaging with them in a personal way.

In doing so, you're pre-warming these people to your services. So, while those you engage with now might not be in a position to elicit your services, by touching base with them regularly you're keeping your firm front-of-mind for when the need for your services does arise.

> **EXPERT TIP: NO.3**
>
> *You can engage with someone in a personal way on social media by observing what they've shown an interest in and suggesting other pieces of branded content that might appeal to their appetite. Or alternatively you can start conversations with people of interest to your firm to build relationships, and wait for them to become fruitful later on down the line.*

PROMOTE YOUR CONTENT (EVENTS, BLOGS, PODCASTS)

So often we see clients who have content just sitting on their website, housed on their navigation as *'blogs', 'insights', 'collateral'* or *'our thoughts'*. What they don't realise is that unless you're one of the top five professional services firms, it's unlikely that people are going to scour your website looking for content. This leaves these valuable resources sat on the shelf, rather than maximising their mileage.

Social media platforms like LinkedIn, Facebook and Twitter offer the perfect opportunity to make more out of this content. By posting them on social media you can drive new traffic there and get them seen by more people.

When you're thinking about what content to post on social media, consider what people are looking for on the platform. For example, people on Facebook want to engage with bite-size content whereas on LinkedIn people are more willing to get stuck into longer articles.

"FACEBOOK SENDS MORE SOCIAL MEDIA TRAFFIC TO SHORTER NEWS ARTICLES THAN LONGER STORIES"

- Pew Research Center, 2016

PLANNING AHEAD AND SCHEDULING

The simplest way to ensure you're posting regular, quality content with consistent messages, and leveraging the content you already have, is to come up with a social schedule for what you plan to post and when.

With all our clients, we suggest drawing up a social media content calendar to capitalise on current trends and properly prioritise your campaigns. These social calendars are usually in a diary-style calendar and include:

- Key dates in the professional services industry
- Dates of any external facing campaigns
- Key dates for clients

These dates serve as the 'bones' of a social media schedule and should be fleshed out with the promotion of existing assets, industry relevant statistics, client testimonials and interesting, industry relevant news.

Having a social schedule—which acts as a guide for what you're going to talk about and when—will **increase** your content's exposure and **limit** repetition. Social schedules are designed to be flexible, with the best ones leaving room for reactive posts when the industry requires it.

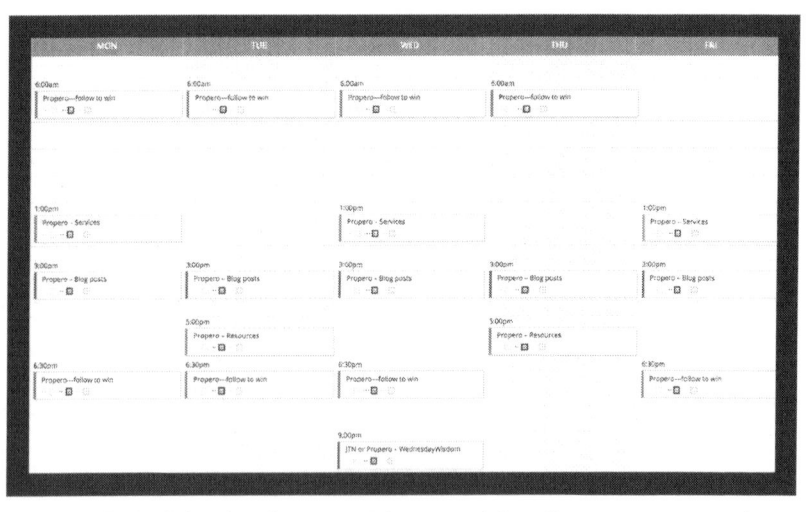

Social schedule taken from Meet Edgar, a social media management tool.

Once you've drawn up your own social calendar, you can save time by automating your posts using a social automation platform, scheduling them to be posted at specific or optimum times of the day. This tactic will not only help you to better leverage your resources but it will also help you to avoid a last-minute scramble for share-worthy content.

IMAGERY

Because social media offers consumers easily digestible content, individuals tend to follow a vast number of accounts. Posts from all of these accounts will be shown on their 'home feed', which means your firm is constantly competing to be seen.

> **TWEETS WITH IMAGES RECEIVE 18% MORE CLICKS, 89% MORE FAVOURITES, AND 150% MORE RETWEETS**
>
> *- Tap Snap, 2016*

Visual content performs 4.4 times better than text-based content on social media, so it's important to master the art of imagery if you want your profile to stand out above the rest (Tap Snap, 2016).

EXPERT TIP: NO.4

We recommend using strong and recognisable images, as they will help your firm to get information across in a way that requires minimum effort from the consumer.

Remember that humans process images a *lot* faster (60,000 times) than text (FifteenDesign, 2016), so if you have text based content that can be represented in a visual way, it will increase the engagement and reach of your post.

FOLLOW THE 90:10 RULE

Originally the 80:20 rule, this simple ratio should form the basis of all your firm's social posting. Social media shouldn't be used for hard sales messages. It's where your ideal clients go to read information that interests them, so if you bombard them with posts about your firm they'll keep scrolling.

Remember these key facts when you're posting *anything* on social media:

- **90%** of your content should be **what the reader wants to see** (i.e. answers to thier burning buying questions)

- **10%** of content should be **what you want the reader to see** (i.e. your products or services)

Striking this balance will ensure your firm's brand is appealing, your audience is more engaged and you have the opportunity to put your services in front of them in a way that resonates.

CASE STUDY

While PwC IS known as one of the most prestigious accounting firms in the world, it wasn't known for its social media campaigns...

Until it championed its 'Ballot Briefcase' campaign in the lead up to the Academy Awards, that is.

When PwC's marketing team sat down to brainstorm how they could reposition the firm's branding to appeal to a younger talent demographic, a social media campaign was the obvious answer. But what did an accounting firm have to offer the millennial generation, when there were innumerable other social media campaigns out there targeting the very same people?

→

The firm, that had managed the ballots for the Oscars ceremony for 82 years, decided to run a campaign (using a host of social media channels) to create a buzz about its involvement. But, instead of pushing the firm's brand, they decided to let the briefcase and its involvement in the awards take the front seat.

The result? The campaign increased PwC's social impressions by almost 136x on Twitter and won them the Shorty Award for the best B2B campaign on social media.

By using a topic that would resonate with the audience they were targeting, and without pushing a hard sales message, PwC successfully engaged millennials AND created huge visibility for the brand.

DEMONSTRATE A STRONG, PROFESSIONAL BRAND AND AUTHORITATIVE VOICE

Social media channels offer an inexpensive platform for you to position your business as a leader in your industry—so it's worth spending the time to make sure yours is representing your firm the way you want it to.

Most website components are static. You may occasionally post a blog or update your 'about us' page when someone new joins the team, but on the whole, it's likely your website doesn't see a lot of change. Social platforms however give your business the unique opportunity to talk about industry issues in real-time, which gives your firm a louder voice in the industry.

Think of your social media profiles as a stage, where other likeminded business audiences are ready and waiting to listen to your insights and consume your content. Your business has unique expertise to offer and knowledge to share, so—to position your firm as a leader in your industry—it's vital that you 'speak' with confidence.

Because, as the old saying goes:

"How do you expect others to believe you, if you don't believe in yourself first?"

It might be cliché but, there's an important lesson to learn. If you don't show that you believe in your brand, it's going to be difficult to persuade others to buy into it.

So, talk with authority by replacing words like: *'sometimes', 'it can', 'usually', 'quite effective'*, with concrete words like: *'will', 'leads to', 'as a result'* and *'directly impacts'*, to better showcase your firm's knowledge and experience in its sector.

(For more information on how to demonstrate authority through language, and the difference language makes to people's behaviour, consult Chapter 3 of our Content Marketing book).

LISTEN TO THE CONVERSATIONS HAPPENING IN YOUR INDUSTRY

Being able to see the real-time conversations happening in your industry is a huge benefit of social media.

Aligning the interests of the industry with the content and positioning of your firm's services is what top professional services firms do and how they reap the highest engagement. They use the visibility that social media gives to influence the content they produce.

It's called 'social listening', and it's just another way of researching the market, monitoring what your prospects say about your industry online *and* initiating informed conversations with them...

Delving a little deeper, social media enables:

1. Salespeople to see what prospects are saying about their brand and competitors
2. Marketers to generate new leads, by using the platforms to find opportunities and determine the names of the true buyers and decision makers inside organisations
3. Businesses to build deeper relationships with existing clients, driving them to purchase again. and again.

So how do you leverage social listening to help identify your best prospects?

Social media can be used to identify your best prospects by creating consumer profiles. Leverage the content overload to gain a better idea of who to target, where they are, what industries they're in and what they're saying about your industry.

"Consumer profiling is a way of categorically defining your prospect to better target them based on their individual characteristics. You can then use this information to offer a superior service that speaks to your prospects on a personal level." (Propero Partners, 2016).

Define your best prospects by:

1. **Demographic** – age, industry, job role, experience
2. **Location** – where they live, where they work
3. **Psychographic characteristics** – opinions, attitudes, interests, lifestyle
4. **Buying patterns** – where they buy, how they buy, amount, frequency, timing.

You can collect a lot of this information *right now*. So leave cold calling to traditional salespeople, boost your consumer knowledge using social listening and consumer profiling, and initiate informed conversations with your ideal prospects, today.

Using organic traction (such as hashtags) and trending topics to boost the exposure of your content is a technique we call 'riding the media wave.' By capitalising on trends and the interests of your followers, your posts will be put in front of more people and gain maximum exposure—helping your content to reach a larger number of people and giving you the best chance of higher engagement rates.

For better *or* for worse, social media marketing is here to stay—but it's how you use it that dictates how successful it will be for your firm.

EXPERT TIP: NO.5

You don't need to rewrite content based on what's trending, however you should highlight the link between the content you're promoting and the trending topic at hand. Doing this will increase your engagement with minimal input.

CHAPTER 4

SOCIAL MEDIA TAKEAWAYS TO ACTION TODAY

To gain a better understanding of what content you should post on social media to facilitate your business' growth, here are some essential *"dos and don'ts"* to maximise your efforts:

Do... offer your opinion on emerging trends. This is a great way to position yourself as an expert while informing your audience of updates in their industry. You will boost engagement by showcasing your expertise and offering valuable advice on issues that actually affect your clients.

Do... give the kind of information that genuinely helps your clients and prospects without them needing to pay you—offer just enough free counsel without giving away your 'intellectual property'. This way, you're not undervaluing your services, and your serious enquiries will understand that to reach a comprehensive solution, they need to work with you. Remember, the majority of prospective clients aren't ready to buy immediately, so this approach will help to keep your firm front-of-mind for when they are.

> **71% OF CONSUMERS ARE MORE LIKELY TO PURCHASE BASED ON SOCIAL MEDIA REFERRALS.**
>
> *- Hubspot, 2017*

Do... be selective about what you post to ensure your prospective clients only see you at your best. Whether you're writing an opinion piece or sharing a link to a relevant article, remember the following: ***think mindshare, not mindless***. This will help you to filter value from nonsense.

Don't... follow the example of fledgling businesses before you. While it may be tempting to post a mindless commentary on your latest business offering, spamming your followers will only force them to disconnect.

Think beyond the sale—why should your audience choose to work with you over your competitors? **Don't tell them you're an expert, show them.** Demonstrate your experience and know-how with topical posts and opinion pieces to promote the value of your expertise, without over-selling the features that prospective clients have learned to tune-out.

It's important to remember that today's consumer is less likely to engage with you if what you post lacks thought. And that means posting trivial updates for the sake of having a consistent, up-to-date feed is MORE damaging than having no online presence at all. Instead, use online platforms to engage with your followers and to start a conversation. That's why social media is so effective at helping you to learn more about prospective clients and how they respond to your services, and then using that momentum to convert them into new-business.

In the following chapters we will discuss kick-starting your digital marketing activity, from setting goals, to choosing both organic and paid solutions to achieve them and knowing whether you're best placed to do the work yourself...

CHAPTER 5

ACHIEVE YOUR BUSINESS GOALS WITH MARKETING

Now that you have a fundamental understanding of social media, with that, one piece of the digital marketing puzzle has fallen into place for you. Now it's time to boost your firm's exposure online with what you've read so far and to understand the many other marketing strategies you can utilise to achieve your business goals.

(For more information on upcoming books in the "Marketing for Non-Marketers" series, visit the Propero website.)

Before you decide between hiring your neighbour's son who has a marketing degree, enquiring at a marketing agency for some direction, or just getting started yourself, consider what you hope to achieve from your marketing efforts.

Many firms assume they should start marketing first and that their goals and target audience will become apparent once it's up and running. While this approach can eventually help you identify 'hand-raisers' who are interested in your firm's services, it often means putting a lot of time and effort into random activities until one of them happens to work. We call these activities "random acts of marketing".

WILL REFRESHING YOUR WEBSITE AUTOMATICALLY DRIVE TRAFFIC TO IT AND GENERATE NEW BUSINESS ENQUIRIES?
NOT IF THEY DON'T KNOW IT EXISTS.

These random acts are *never* measurable and often firms spend so much money on marketing activities that yield no results, that they then feel burned by marketing and decide it's a waste of resources.

Truth be told, this type of marketing IS a waste of your time and money. However, with a structured plan, you will be able to produce marketing strategies that work.

You can begin to inform your firm's marketing approach with four simple questions...

QUESTION 1

WHO ARE YOU TARGETING?

The big question here, is how do you avoid random acts of marketing and start implementing marketing strategies that produce measurable results? The first step is to know **who your target audience is.**

> **EXPERT TIP NO.6**
>
> WHO IS YOUR IDEAL CLIENT? BRAINSTORM WITH YOUR TEAM...
>
> WHO ARE WE TRYING TO REACH? HOW CAN WORKING WITH YOUR FIRM BENEFIT THEIR BUSINESS? WHY WOULD THEY WANT TO WORK WITH YOU SPECIFICALLY?

Random acts of marketing tend to happen when a company doesn't know who their target audience is. Once you've narrowed down and identified your "right-fit" client, your marketing efforts can specifically target the right people, with the right job title, in the right industries. Why waste time marketing to anyone and everyone, when you could avoid the time-wasters and only target eager prospects who would benefit from, and are genuinely interested in, working with you?

QUESTION 2

WHAT ARE YOUR GOALS?

Once you know who you are targeting, the second step is to know your goals. Now you know who you are reaching, you can think about what you're trying to achieve from your marketing efforts.

Is your objective to gain new business enquiries? Are you trying to build and establish new relationships with partner companies? Increase new business by 20%?

Whatever your goals may be, your marketing efforts will start and end with them—you will measure the results you've achieved against the goals you've set, and revisit those goals over time to ensure they remain relevant.

EXPERT TIP: NO.7

To take your goals a step further, start by creating **SMART** goals. These types of goals are:

Specific
Measurable
Achievable
Relevant
Time-bound

Take the goal "gain new business enquiries" and make it SMART: If this was a goal for a leadership consulting company in London, it wouldn't be specific enough to achieve growth. To hit the SMART criteria, we would change it to: "gain 5 new business enquiries (measurable and achievable) from one-to-one leadership consulting clients (specific and relevant) in London over the next 2 months (time-bound)."

With specific criteria that are measurable, achievable, and relevant for your firm, you will be able to set a goal that is attainable within a certain timeframe. Knowing your target audience and then creating goals from there allows you to lay the foundation for your successful marketing plan. Whether you plan to create your own marketing strategy, or choose to outsource, it is key to consider your SMART goals before you begin.

QUESTION 3

WHAT STRATEGIES WILL REACH YOUR TARGET AUDIENCE?

After you've established SMART goals, **the next step is to develop marketing strategies.** These are the tactics you will use to achieve your objectives.

Some examples of digital marketing strategies (outside of the social media foundation you've been reading about) are: Content Marketing, Paid Social Media Advertising, Search Engine Marketing (SEM), Online Display Advertising, Retargeting Advertising (sometimes referred to as remarketing), Email Marketing, Events, LinkedIn InMail Campaigns, Video Advertisements (such as those on YouTube), and Direct Mail Marketing. Yes – Digital marketing is vast!

Depending on your target audience and the goals you've set, you will choose different strategies to reach them. For instance, say the goal is "5 new business enquiries from one-to-one leadership consulting clients in London over the next 2 months". One strategy that would work for this goal is paid social media advertising as the advertising platforms within social media platforms allow your firm to target specific individuals based on their seniority, industry, interests and location.

To increase your firm's exposure and help you to achieve your goal even more successfully employ more than one strategy per goal (it's best to consider a variety of different strategies that make sense for a particular goal, even if you're not necessarily going to work on all of them). Along with paid social advertising, to gain "5 new business enquiries from one-to-one leadership consulting clients in London over the next 2 months" your team could also put into place retargeting ads, host an event, and set up a LinkedIn InMail Campaign with organic social media promotion.

QUESTION 4

WHAT INITIATIVES WILL YOU USE TO ACTION YOUR STRATEGIES?

Once you know who you're targeting, your goals, and you've determined the best strategies to reach your target audience, you then **establish your initiatives**. Initiatives elaborate on the tactics you plan to use to reach your objective so that the information becomes highly actionable.

There are three primary considerations for when you are developing your initiatives: target audience (who), the delivery platform (how), and the topic (what).

EXPERT TIP: NO.8

Say one of your strategies is retargeting, one initiative would be: ad design, copy, and implementation for display ads that appear on a prospect's browser after they've left your website to keep your firm's services front-of-mind. Retargeting campaigns will direct traffic to specific services pages and a content piece that you've recently added to your website.

Now that you've planned your strategies and initiatives you can measure them against your goals.

Will they help your firm to reach your target audience?

- Is your messaging relevant and prompting prospects to engage with you?

- If the answer is yes, you are doing a great job. If not, you now have a baseline to measure your marketing against and an opportunity to reassess before you get started.

Now what? Well, since you know who you are targeting, your goals, strategies, and initiatives, you will no longer be running campaigns with your fingers crossed hoping that they will work. *No more random acts of marketing.*

By setting strategies with your audience and your services in mind, you will see the fruit of your marketing efforts. You will be able to see the cost of a campaign and cross reference that with how many leads you've generated from the different strategies you've put into place.

THIS IS THE MEASURABLE MARKETING YOU'VE BEEN LOOKING FOR.

This doesn't mean that every one of your initiatives will work perfectly the first time you put them into place. There will be consistent tweaking that needs to be done. If you are running paid social ads on LinkedIn and they aren't performing, you need to ask yourself: is the messaging engaging your target audience? Is LinkedIn the right platform for these ads? (Maybe Twitter or Facebook would reach your audience better.) Successful marketing is adaptable—you need to look at changing the language, branding, platform, or images to reach your target audience.

Once you've established what works (and what doesn't) to reach your target audience, and ultimately your goals, you will begin engaging with interested prospects. With your expert targeting in place, eager prospects will be coming to you, already interested in your services. At this point, instead of speaking to anyone and everyone who reaches you, remember your target audience and **engage with your "right-fit" clients**.

If you are trying to reach CEOs of private equity firms in the UK, but you get a call from a Head of School in Canada who is also interested in your services, focus your attention on the CEOs. Know who your ideal client is and be intentional about who you speak to. This way, you won't waste time with people who you know from experience can't afford your services or are a wrong-fit, and those who you can't generate great success for.

Let's recap. Many firms want to use marketing to grow, but start off on the wrong foot with "random acts of marketing." Instead of getting started with just any marketing activity, determining a target audience and setting goals, strategies, and initiatives allows you to establish **marketing that is measurable, marketing that works**. Once prospects begin to engage, its up to the company to partner with "right-fit" clients and repel the prospects who are time-wasters.

From here, you will either be able to guide your own marketing efforts, or you'll have a better understanding of what to look for in a marketing proposal from an agency who is equipped to do it for you.

CHAPTER 6

KNOW WHEN TO STOP DOING IT YOURSELF

Now that you're nearing the end of this book, you should be feeling more comfortable using social media to boost your firm's online presence, and the processes and activities that fall under the umbrella of _organic social media marketing_.

You may also be feeling motivated to go away and start implementing the non-negotiables that you've learned about in this book, so that you can start seeing greater returns on your social media profiles.

However, implementation and the ongoing management of it does come with its own demands (regardless of how equipped you now are to tackle it all yourself). Namely, the strain it can put on already stretched resources (which are typically in very short supply in professional services firms).

That's why it's important to ask yourself these questions: do you map out and implement a social media strategy yourself, or find a marketing agency to do it for you? And if you decide to go with the latter, what should you look for in a right-fit agency?

If you have bought and read any of the other books in Propero's *Marketing for Non-Marketers* series, then you will be familiar with what WE think a leading marketing agency looks like. But, if this is your first book, then let us walk you through the process of how to identify what the right support for you looks like.

For anyone who knows that they want to do their own marketing, skip to page 77.

To start, you'll need to do some googling and asking around to find agencies that have worked with clients like your firm before. Make a shortlist of agencies that you'd like to work with, and then if possible, meet with these candidate agencies in person—meeting face-to-face gives you a good sense of the type of agency you'll be partnering with. It's always best to find people you enjoy working with and speaking to, especially if you are going to be working closely with them to grow your business. When you meet (or talk over the phone, as meetings aren't always feasible), explain your company's target audience and goals. Then ask the agencies you've spoken with to make some recommendations based on the clients you'd like to target and the growth you'd like to achieve.

Once you've explained your business and who your ideal prospect is, it's time to ask the agency to explain their process and how they are going to achieve your goals. You now know how to lay the foundation for a successful marketing strategy and should use what you've learned to make sure the agency you want to partner with leverages sound marketing strategies.

In the preliminary meetings, here are a few things to ask the agency:

1. Can they show you success stories and tangible, measurable results from the campaigns they've run for other clients? (Through reports, data, case studies etc.)

2. Have they worked with similar clients before?

3. Do they have any social proof? (For example, testimonials from reputable clients, any awards, are they quoted in any established publications etc.)

4. Can they send examples of the type of work they are offering to complete for you? (Note that this can be anonymised.)

5. How do they measure their marketing? And how do they calculate ROI?

These are just a few examples of questions to ask an agency before you sign on the dotted line. These questions give you a quick insight into the kind of agency you're dealing with—an established agency will be able to answer these questions with ease, however agencies that are "all talk and no action" will have a difficult time giving you proof of their "great" work.

If you ask for examples of anonymised content and the agency sends them over to you right away, then you know they follow through, plus they have examples of good work on hand. This is early evidence that they do what they say they are going to do. However, if you ask for examples and are given nothing, or are given an excuse, then you can expect the agency to continue to work with excuses and promises they can't keep. They are not the right partner for you.

Asking an agency about how they measure their marketing (or asking about ROI) will show you if they are working to business metrics, or if they are working to vanity statistics (in other words, statistics that seem great, look really nice on paper, but mean nothing to the growth of your business). You want to work with an agency that measures their efforts against metrics that grow your company (or any metric that helps you reach the goals you've set). If they propose a plan that looks like many instances of "random acts of marketing," they are not the agency to invest your time and money in. However, if they measure their marketing against metrics that matter (reaching your goals, getting a certain number of leads, booking a set number of meetings, etc.) they are an agency to consider working with.

Once you get the answers to your questions, and shortlist the agencies you'd like to move forward with, it's time to give them the green light so that they can send you proposals. These bids will outline how the agency will achieve your goals and the specific approaches they will take to do so. Each of these proposals will promise the moon and you'll wonder why you didn't bring a marketing agency on board sooner.

To choose between agencies that all make themselves sound spectacular, make sure to read between the lines to define what they're REALLY going to do for you. If you've been asking the right questions, trying to understand their process, and reiterating that you expect to receive measurable results that will aid in business growth, you will be able to determine whether or not that particular proposal will provide a worthy return on investment for your business.

From there, you'll decide which agency works best for you—if there's more than one on your shortlist then it could come down to simple things when making the final decision, where they're based or how attentive they've been.

Now that you've done your due diligence and found the agency that works for you, it's time for the agency to get started on the work they've promised to complete for you.

Since you've explained your goals and who your target audience is, the agency will put the strategies and initiatives into place to help grow your firm. Getting to this stage requires a lot of time and effort on your part, which is why during the onboarding process, you can take a back seat until the work gets underway. The agency will need your approval on copy and creative direction (depending on the specific project they may need more feedback from you), but the bulk of the initial setup work is now their job to execute. They will put the strategies in place to generate new enquiries for your firm (or drive traffic to your site, or book in more meetings).

Once right-fit leads begin to flow through, **it's your turn to take those prospects and convert them into clients...**

FOR ANYONE WHO SKIPPED THE AGENCY SECTION, JOIN BACK IN HERE...

This next step is *very* important and requires time and attention (for those doing their own marketing AND for those using an agency). You need to take those leads your agency has passed onto you (or that you've collected, for those of you who have set up your own online marketing) and nurture them into clients. Your marketing efforts should be generating prospects who've shown interest in your services and you need to know what to do with them once they are in your hands.

> **SO OFTEN AT THIS STAGE, COMPANIES THINK THEY AREN'T GETTING THE RIGHT KIND OF LEADS AND THEIR MARKETING ISN'T WORKING. BUT IT'S OFTEN BECAUSE THEY DON'T KNOW WHAT TO DO ONCE THEY HAVE THEM.**

This process starts with receiving the lead's contact information, and ends with them signing on the dotted line to become your client. That includes nurturing them, keeping in contact with them, and not letting them go cold. Depending on your contract with your agency, they may help you with this by creating follow-up email sequences and phone scripts for you to use, sending out direct mail to engaged prospects, and setting up retargeting campaigns to keep your company front-of-mind. Regardless of how much they are doing on your behalf, once they give you a name, email address and/or phone number, **your team needs to proactively reach out.**

> # THEY'VE DONE THEIR JOB, NOW IT'S TIME FOR YOU TO DO YOURS.

If your marketing team has set up ad campaigns that encourage potential clients to call, make sure you have your team trained and ready to answer the phone. If your campaigns encourage leads to send an email, make sure your team is equipped to answer within 24 hours so those leads don't go cold. These things may sound self-explanatory, but so often leads are given to companies that don't have the resources to follow up, or don't have the right procedures in place to make sure leads aren't falling through the cracks.

Prospects will react differently depending on how you choose to get in contact with them. The goal with generating enquiries is to nurture good relationships with prospects and turn them into paying clients. To do this, know your audience (what they will and won't respond well to) and engage with them accordingly.

If a great lead doesn't respond at first, they may need a few more touch points with your firm before they speak directly to you. Create reasons to contact them off the back of their initial engagement.

If a prospect downloads a piece of gated content and leaves their email address, there are a couple of approaches to consider when reaching out to them...

- Ask their opinion on the download and whether they have any questions

- Send them a blog that is related to the content they downloaded and explain how this information will really help them

- Ask the prospect if they'd like to get on the phone and discuss the information you've sent them.

If the lead is engaged (they downloaded a guide or showed interest on your website), but not ready to buy into your services just yet, don't throw their contact details away. Just because the lead isn't ready to buy now, doesn't mean they will never need your services.

BUT if it's been a while since your first contact don't be afraid to check in with them...

- Is there an event you think they would benefit from attending? Send them an invite

- Is there an industry update that your potential client would benefit from knowing about? Write a blog post about it and use that as an excuse to send them an email.

Creating relevant reasons to contact potential clients is a great way to re-engage with leads who are eager, but who weren't ready to buy a few months prior.

The key here is to send prospects ***relevant*** materials and to not let them go cold. Instead of thinking about all the ways you can show off your services, think about your ideal client's pain points and send them articles, news and event invitations that offer solutions to those problems. This is a great way to start a conversation about their needs, to develop a relationship with them which will position your firm front-of-mind when they need your services most.

When done well, **marketing will help your firm to be present in the right places to attract the right people.**

Whether you decide to invest in a marketing agency or pursue marketing in-house, the most successful marketing works to achieve your firm's individual business goals (this means avoiding vanity stats that don't create new business opportunities for your firm). With ROI-driven, measurable marketing campaigns in place you'll begin to attract prospects who are interested in the services you offer. And with a continued focus on what's working, the leads generated will become more 'right-fit' for your firm. When this happens, it's time for you to get in touch to showcase your knowledge and experience in relevant industries/situations to close more prospects into paying clients and grow your business.

It may sound simple when written in black and white, but **don't underestimate the power of a good marketing campaign, or a *bad* one.**

SOCIAL MEDIA CALENDAR

This calendar is not to scale. Download the full version here:
https://properopartners.com/social-media-calendar

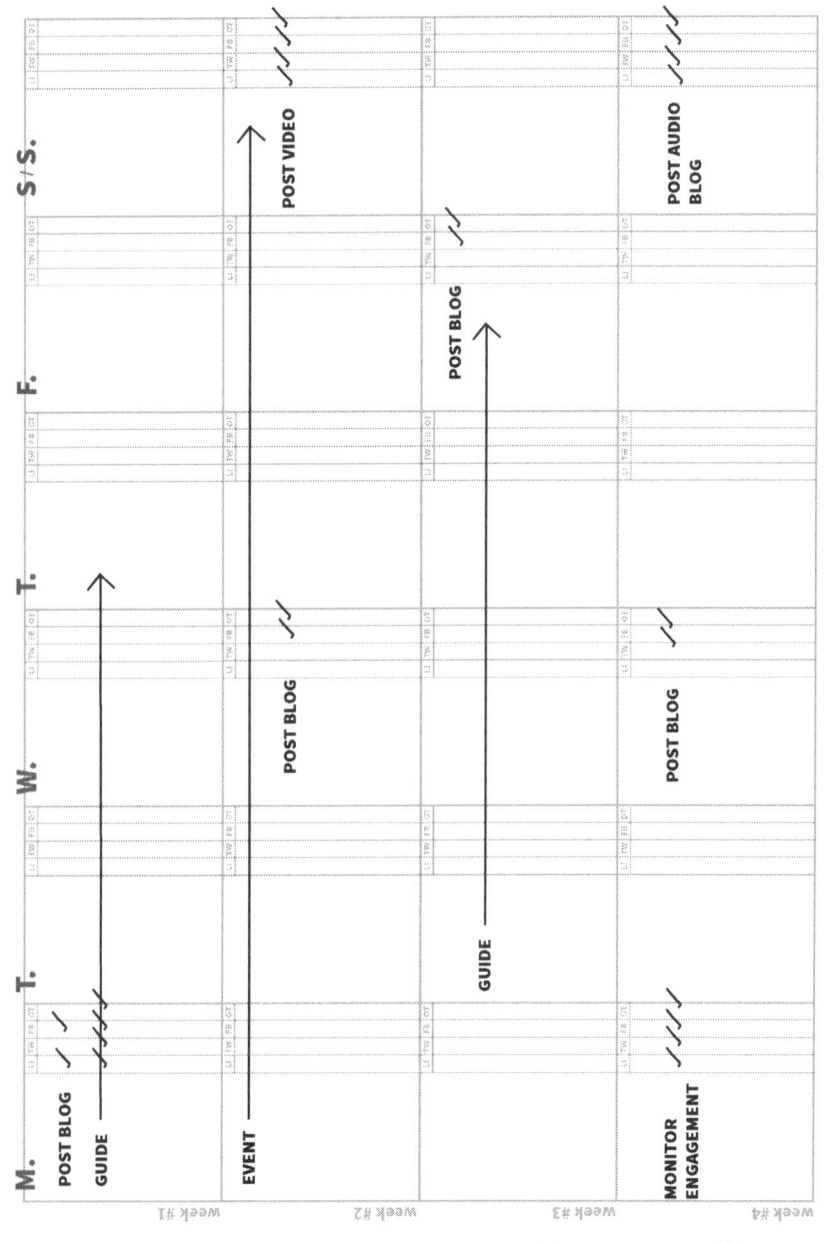

	M.	T.	W.	T.	F.	S/S.
week #1	POST BLOG / GUIDE					
week #2	EVENT		POST BLOG			POST VIDEO
week #3		GUIDE			POST BLOG	
week #4	MONITOR ENGAGEMENT		POST BLOG			POST AUDIO BLOG

FROM: 12/2/18   TO: 16/2/18

REFERENCES

ABA TechReport. (2014). Blogging and Social Media. [online] American Bar Association, Available at: https://www.americanbar.org/groups/law_practice/publications/techreport/2014.html [Accessed 5 Dec. 2017].

Business.linkedin.com. (2017). LinkedIn Company Page Best Practices | LinkedIn Marketing Solutions. [online] Available at: https://business.linkedin.com/marketing-solutions/company-pages/best-practices [Accessed 11 Oct. 2017].

Ewing, M. (2017). 71% More Likely to Purchase Based on Social Media Referrals [Infographic]. [online] Blog.hubspot.com. Available at: https://blog.hubspot.com/blog/tabid/6307/bid/30239/71-more-likely-to-purchase-based-on-social-media-referrals-infographic.aspx [Accessed 5 Oct. 2017].

FifteenDesign. (2016). Why Using Imagery On Social Media Is The Key For Engagement. [online] Available at: https://www.fifteendesign.co.uk/blog/why-using-imagery-on-social-media-is-the-key-for-engagement/ [Accessed 6 Oct. 2017].

Fontein, D. (2016). The Ultimate List of LinkedIn Statistics for Business. [online] Hootsuite Social Media Management Available at: https://blog.hootsuite.com/linkedin-statistics-business/# [Accessed 3 Nov. 2017].

Maersk Line. (2017). Facebook Profile. [online] Available at: https://www.facebook.com/MaerskLine [Accessed 21 Oct. 2017].

Matsa, K. (2016). Facebook, Twitter play different roles in connecting mobile readers to news. [online] Pew Research Center. Available at: http://www.pewresearch.org/fact-tank/2016/05/09/facebook-twitter-mobile-news/ [Accessed 9 Nov. 2017].

Meltwater. (2015). 20 Brilliant B2B Digital Business and Marketing Stats and Facts. [online] Available at: https://www.meltwater.com/blog/20-brilliant-b2b-marketing-and-digital-business-stats-and-facts/ [Accessed 19 Sep. 2017].

Noble, J. (2016). Interview with James Noble for Propero Partners' blog, 28 September. [online] Available at: http://www.properopartners.com/social-media-prospects-online/ [Accessed 10 Oct. 2017].

Oxford Dictionary | English. (2017). Social media | Definition of social media in English by Oxford Dictionary. [online] Available at: https://en.oxforddictionaries.com/definition/social_media [Accessed 1 Dec. 2017].

Propero Partners (2016). Building Authority: Driving Online Revenue With Social Media | Propero Partners. [online] Propero Partners. Available at: http://www.properopartners.com/building-authority-driving-online-revenue-with-social-media/ [Accessed 14 Aug. 2017].

Propero Partners (2017). State of Digital Marketing in the Professional Services Industry. [online] London: Propero Partners, pp.17,54-55. Available at: http://www.properopartners.com/2017-report/ [Accessed 29 Aug. 2017].

PwC. (2017). Twitter Profile. [online] Available at: https://twitter.com/pwc_uk?lang=en [Accessed 21 Oct. 2017].

Roxburgh, H. (2014). Three quarters of accountants use social media | ICAEW Economia. [online] Economia.icaew.com. Available at: http://economia.icaew.com/en/news/january-2014/three-quarters-of-accountants-use-social-media [Accessed 24 Nov. 2017].

Statista. (2017). Most famous social network sites worldwide as of September 2017, ranked by number of active users (in millions). [online] Available at: https://www.statista.com/statistics/272014/global-social-networks-ranked-by-number-of-users/ [Accessed 8 Nov. 2017].

Tapsnap.net. (2016). 5 Stats Explaining the Importance of Visual Content on Social Media. [online] Available at:https://tapsnap.net/blog/5-stats-explaining-the-importance-of-visual-content-on-social-media/ [Accessed 13 Sep. 2017].

Printed in Great Britain
by Amazon